and Just Plain Dangerous

World War II

John
Townsend

illustrated by
Matt Lilly

EDGE

FRANKLIN WATTS

LONDON•SYDNEY

First published in 2013 by Franklin Watts

Created and developed by Taglines Creative Limited
Text by John Townsend
Illustrations and layout by Matt Lilly
Cover design by Cathryn Gilbert

Franklin Watts
338 Euston Road London NW1 3BH

Franklin Watts Australia
Level 17/207 Kent Street, Sydney, NSW 2000

A CIP catalogue record for this book
is available from the British Library.

(ebook) ISBN: 978 1 4451 2240 3
(PB) ISBN: 978 1 4451 2194 9
(Library ebook) ISBN: 978 1 4451 2583 1

1 3 5 7 9 10 8 6 4 2

Picture credits:
p.6 Pictorial Press Ltd/Alamy; p.8 Jim Vallee/Shutterstock;
p.11 Alexia Khruscheva/Shutterstock; p.22 Andy Lidstone/Shutterstock;
p.24 hauhu/Shutterstock; p.31 Viorel Sima/Shutterstock;
p.32 thieury/Shutterstock; p.34 Image Asset Management Ltd/Alamy;
p.47 Alexia Khruscheva/Shutterstock; p.53 Kuttelvaserova
Stuchelova/Shutterstock; p.60 Eric Isselee/Shutterstock;
p.62 Bruce MacQueen/Shutterstock; p.63 Vitalli Hulai/Shutterstock;
p.64 John Carnemolla/Shutterstock; p.65 AnetaPics/Shutterstock;
p.70 Sergey Kamshylin/Shutterstock; p.72 Uwe Bumann/Shutterstock;
pp.66-67 Sergey Kamshylin/Shutterstock; p.82 Alexia Khruscheva/Shutterstock;
p.85 Krasowit/Shutterstock; p.86 Pan Xunbin/Shutterstock

Every attempt has been made to clear copyright on the photographs
reproduced in this book. Any omissions, please apply to the
Publisher for rectification.

Printed and bound by CPI Group (UK) Ltd, Croydon, CR0 4YY

Franklin Watts is
a division of Hachette Children's Books,
an Hachette UK company.

www.hachette.co.uk

THIS BOOK IS FUN!

It could seriously change the way you think about history!

What do you think grown-ups will make of this book?

I bet they read it secretly under the bedclothes!

CONTENTS

Read on or else vee vill come to get you!

Chapter 1
Wicked World War Worries

Only 21 years after World War I ended, an even greater war started — World War II. From 1939 to 1945 between 50 and 70 million people died. Half of these were women and children. World War II cost more money, damaged more property, caused more refugees and killed more people than any other war in history.

My name is Adolf Hitler, and I want to make Germany great again... oh yes, and take over the world.

For those in the Second
World War

There was madness and
danger galore.

And fear so extreme,

Get ready to scream...

Read on if you dare to
know more!

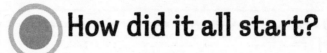

How did it all start?

In 1918, Germany was beaten in World War I. It had to give away a lot of land and was not allowed to have any armed forces. That angered many German people. In 1933, they voted for a new leader called Adolf Hitler, who called his Nazi government the 'Third Reich'. Hitler planned to build the strongest army ever and take land from other countries nearby and around the world.

Hmm, I need a symbol to represent my Nazi Party. Ah, this swastika will do nicely.

The madness begins

On Friday 1st September, 1939, an invasion force
of over one million German soldiers marched
into Poland. The maddest, 'baddest' and most
dangerous war of modern times had begun.

It's war!

Blimey – where is everyone? Was it something I said?

The British Prime Minister, Neville Chamberlain, told Hitler to get out of Poland fast! Hitler didn't, so Britain declared war on Germany on 3rd September, 1939. Everyone dreaded what would happen next. But everything went quiet — nothing happened. That all changed, though. Hitler went berserk! The world would never, ever be the same again...

WORLD WAR DECLARED OFFICIAL

World War II involved over 60 countries.

BADDIES: the Axis countries. Main leaders:

Adolf Hitler, Germany

Emperor Hirohito, Japan

Benito Mussolini, Italy

GOODIES: the Allies. Main leaders:

Joseph Stalin, Russia

Franklin D. Roosevelt, USA

Winston Churchill, Britain

Hitler  the Soap

So who did what in World War II? Find out in our exciting new soap starting on page 20.

Cast list:

Adolf Hitler	German leader or Führer
Hermann Göering	Nazi military leader
Joseph Göebbels	Hitler's Minister of Propaganda
Winston Churchill	British Prime Minister
Clement Attlee	Leader of the UK Labour Party
King George VI	British king
Queen Elizabeth	Wife of the king
Franklin D. Roosevelt	US President
Benito Mussolini	Italian dictator

Plus evacuees, a Tiger tank, a German Shepherd dog called Blondi and a gang of hungry sharks.

Hitler – the Soap,
CANINE AUDITIONS
THIS WAY

Chapter 2
MAD Moments

During World War II and ever since, people have wondered whether Hitler was mad. He certainly had crazy ideas, but many of his Nazi Party shared them. In fact, they could be far worse than mad, bad and dangerous — they could be insane, evil and treacherous.

How can I be mad ... I like painting!

Young Hitler, it has to
be said,

Was never quite right
in the head.

How the world would
have changed

If he weren't so deranged,

And he'd taken up
ballet instead!

Batty beliefs

The Nazi Party had strict rules about the way people should live. German women had to be housewives, and the men soldiers and workers.

Women could not wear make-up or expensive clothes and had to wear their hair in plaits or in a bun. Mothers were expected to have at least four children, and then they were given a medal every year on the birthday of Hitler's mother. This was called the 'Mutterkreuz', the Mother's Cross.

I deserve a medal for doing this lot every day...

Nazi nutter

Heinrich Himmler was head of the Gestapo, the dreaded German secret police. He was scary and a bit of a nutcase. He believed the future was ruled by the stars, and his Gestapo meetings were held at night in castles lit by flaming torches. His officers were given leeks and mineral water for breakfast, and he insisted on seating 12 people at his table — to be like King Arthur.

Count Him-ula! I'm bloodthirsty for power ... but keep me away from real blood, it makes me faint...

Hitler youth

All German children aged 6 to 18 had to join scary Nazi youth organisations.

For boys: 6–9 years joined the Pimpfe (Little Fellows); 10–13 year olds joined the Deutsches Jungvolk (German Young People); 14–18 years joined the Hitler Youth.

For girls: 10–14 years joined the Jungmädel (Young Maidens), where they were taught how to become good housewives. Older girls joined the Bund Deutscher Mädel (League of German Maidens), where they trained to be mothers.

The Nazis had their own Christmas wrapping paper decorated with swastikas.

Scary schools

Nazi children were given books telling them to play with guns and enjoy fighting. School textbooks were rewritten so that maths problems became sums about bombing Poland and killing people with disabilities. The school day began with a special 'Heil Hitler' salute. Every time a teacher entered the classroom, everyone had to stand and salute.

I want to be like Hitler.

What, stark raving bonkers?

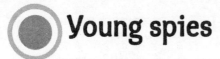

Young spies

Members of the Hitler Youth were told to spy on adults, including their parents. Anything dodgy had to be reported to the Gestapo ... who would do the rest, such as pay the parents a visit, and even take them away.

If I don't get a bedroom upgrade, I'll report them to the Gestapo.

Boy war

At the end of the war, 5,000 Hitler Youth boys with rifles had to defend Berlin from the advancing Russian army. Within five days, 4,500 had been killed or wounded. Some of the boy soldiers were as young as 12. Many Hitler Youth killed themselves rather than be taken alive by the Russians.

JOIN TODAY!

"The weak must be chiselled away. I want young men and women who can suffer pain. A young German must be as swift as a greyhound, as tough as leather and as hard as steel." Adolf Hitler

Hitler  the Soap

Episode 1: Furious Führer

Scene 1: Hitler's HQ with Hermann Göering. Date: 1941.

Action

Hitler: Hermann, have you heard the news?

Göering: Yes, Führer. Your deputy, Rudolf Hess, has just parachuted into Britain and been arrested. He plans to make peace with the Brits.

Hitler: I am furious. I have never been a more furious fuming Führer!

Göering: He went against your orders to talk to that Winston Churchill.

Hitler: Bah, don't mention that man to me. Tell everyone Hess is mad. If he returns to Germany, have him shot.

> Rudolf Hess was imprisoned in the Tower of London. After the war, he was sent to prison in Berlin for his war crimes. He died there at the age of 93 in 1987.

Göering: So, who will take his place, Führer?

Hitler: You, Hermann. But don't upset me or I'll have you shoot yourself.

Göering: We make a good team, my Führer.

Hitler: Of course. You're in charge of my Air Force and you're bonkers like me!

Scene 2: Churchill's HQ, The Cabinet War Rooms, London.

Attlee: Sir Winston, as your deputy prime minister, I need to warn you. Our code breakers say the Nazis are planning to bump you off.

Churchill: And when would that be, Clement? Here, have a piece of chocolate.

Attlee: Stop! Don't touch that bar of chocolate, Prime Minister!

Churchill: Why ever not? You'll be telling me next it's a bomb. Ha, ha, ha!

Attlee: It is! In a luxury wrapper with gold foil.

Churchill: In that case, another mad plot has been FOILED!

I have nothing to offer but blood, toil, tears and chocolate.

Chocolate bombs!

Hitler's bomb-makers coated explosives with a layer of dark chocolate and packaged them in black and gold paper. When the first bit of chocloate was broken off — BOOM!

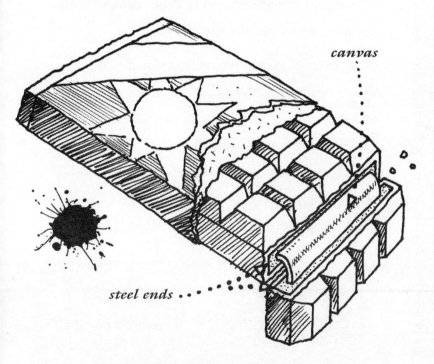

canvas

steel ends

The Nazis planned to get their secret agents in Britain to put the chocolate in Churchill's War Cabinet dining room. The plot was foiled by British spies who discovered the 'death by chocolate' plan!

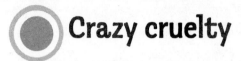

Crazy cruelty

Hitler and the Nazis believed that the Germans were better than all other people. They planned to wipe out other races, especially Jewish people, by sending them all to death camps. Then Germans would become the 'master race'.

Over one million children under 16 died in World War II — not from bombs but because they didn't fit in with Hitler's idea of a 'perfect' German. Families in countries invaded by the Germans were also killed in extermination camps just because they were Jewish. Sending people to these camps became known as the Holocaust.

AUSCHWITZ PRISON CAMP
Over 1 million men, women
and children were killed here.

Team up with friends or try the quiz yourself to see if you would survive in World War II. Add up your scores for each answer. When you've done all the quizzes, check out the final results on page 88.

1. Do you always do as you are told?

A Of course — always

B It all depends

C Hardly ever

2. Would you always salute your country's leader?

A You must be joking!

B Only if I had to

C Yeah, no problem

3. Would you make fun of a crazy crackpot in uniform with daft ideas?

A Maybe

B You bet!

C Not likely

Scores for answers:

1. A = 10   B = 4   C = 1   (Disobeying Nazi leaders could be fatal)
2. A = 0   B = 8   C = 9   (Upsetting the Führer could be fatal)
3. A = 6   B = 0   C = 9   (Making fun of Nazis could be fatal)

Chapter 3

BAD Times

World War II was the first war to bring terror directly to millions of people in their own homes. Air raids with tons of bombs raining down night after night destroyed whole streets and large areas of towns and cities.

Life was full of air-raid sirens, blackouts and fighter planes 'dog-fighting' overhead.

I'm a sitting target...

TOILET

In an outside loo

during the Blitz,

The Deputy Mayor

did the splits

When she fell as she ran,

Shoved her head down

the pan

And screamed at the

Germans: "YOU TWITS!"
(or maybe something ruder)

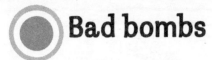

Bad bombs

From September 1940 to May 1941 many British cities were attacked by German planes that dropped bombs in nightly raids known as the Blitz. About 60,000 British people were killed in the Blitz and 87,000 seriously injured. Over 2 million homes were destroyed, as well as many schools.

Some families bought air-raid shelters, such as the Anderson shelter made of corrugated iron sheets, or the cage-like Morrison shelter to use indoors.

Morrison shelter

Dangerous doodlebugs

In 1943, Germany fired thousands of V-I bombs, also known as doodlebugs, on southern England. These were 8-metre missiles that flew at over 600 kph. They were powered by a rocket that suddenly cut out, causing the bomb to fall. The attacks caused widespread panic in London.

People in London often crowded into the Underground railway stations to sleep where it was safe, warm and dry. But some bombs still reached them. In September 1940, a bomb killed 20 people sheltering in Marble Arch station, and 600 people were killed or injured by an explosion at Balham station in October.

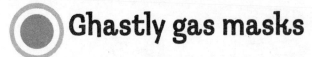

Ghastly gas masks

At the start of the war, the British government feared Hitler would drop poison gas bombs on Britain, so 40 million gas masks were handed out to everyone. Very young children had masks made to look like Mickey Mouse to be less frightening — but they were withdrawn because they cost too much to make.

Oh no, I've got an itchy nose!

Epic evacuations

The fear of bomb and gas attacks in city areas led the British government to evacuate nearly 2 million children to the countryside where they would be safer. They had to leave their parents and get on trains to unknown places. Each child had to be labelled and carry a gas mask.

Country people with spare rooms looked after the evacuees for a small payment. Many 'townie' evacuees were amazed to see cows being milked and vegetables growing in the ground.

All these evacuees make me shudder.

Me too. Now I only make milk shakes!

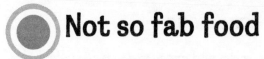

Not so fab food

Britain started to run out of food because German submarines kept sinking ships that were bringing in supplies. To make sure everyone got some basics (cheese, eggs, tea, sugar, butter and meat) the government started rationing in 1940.

Each person was allowed one egg per week, and could buy a packet of dried egg powder to make scrambled egg.

Laying powdered eggs would be so much easier!

Sugar was also in short supply, so all sweets and chocolate were rationed. Children had to get used to lots of turnips, carrots and swedes instead.

Yum!

Gravy legs

Clothes were also rationed. Nylon seamed stockings were the latest women's fashion, but they were hard to find. So instead, some women made a gravy powder paste and used it to colour their legs. Then they drew stocking seams on the backs of their legs. This looked like they were wearing flesh-coloured stockings. Great as long as it didn't rain!

Your legs now have style.

Yeah – and smell like dinner!

Hitler  the Soap

Episode 2: Rallying Royals

Scene 1: Buckingham Palace, London. King George VI and Queen Elizabeth look out over London from their window. Date: 1941.

King: Another terrible raid tonight. I wonder if the palace will be hit again. We had a narrow escape last time.

Queen: Crackers!

King: It's true, dear – don't you remember? We've been hit nine times already.

Queen: Crackers!

King: No, not fire-crackers – huge bombs. They blew out most of the windows on the west wing. The carpets in the corridors got terribly dusty.

Queen: Crackers – get down!

King: *(Diving behind a table)* Where?

Queen: Darling, I was telling Crackers to get down. He's biting the curtains.

King: Ah, the royal corgi!

Queen: Yes, dear. Now then, tomorrow we go and visit people who have been bombed. I want everyone to know I'm standing with them.

King: Crackers!

The next day...

Blimey, Buckingham Palace just got bombed. There's the king and queen.

Was it a bomb or has Crackers been up to his tricks?

Team up with friends or try the quiz yourself to see if you would survive in World War II. Add up your scores for each answer. When you've done all the quizzes, check out the final results on page 88.

1. Do you like to look cool or wear designer clothes?

A You bet

B It doesn't bother me

C Sometimes

---

2. Do you like dried egg and turnips?

A You must be joking!

B Not keen

C Yeah, delicious

---

3. Do you get travel sick, homesick or easily scared of loud noises?

A Probably

B Ooh, what's that bang?

C Not me!

Scores for answers:

1. A = 0   B = 10   C = 4 (You couldn't be fussy about clothes)

2. A = 1   B = 4   C = 9 (You had to eat what was available)

3. A = 4   B = 0   C = 9 (You would have to put up with this and more)

Chapter 4

DANGEROUS and Dodgy Deeds

In the 1940s, unexpected dangers could strike anywhere and at any time. The war leaders had teams of experts trying to work out all the possible dangers. Even so, they could never be prepared for all the nasty surprises in store. Reckless risks, agonising accidents and dreadful disasters were never far away.

Churchill here. This is my new sign for Victory.

Winston Churchill gave
    warnings and speeches

To be brave and 'fight
    on the beaches'.

When the danger was through

He gave thanks for 'the few'
        (as well as the 'phew!')

Making Hitler explode
    in his breeches!

Lights out!

At night during blackouts, no street lights were on, and houses had curtains to stop light showing outside. This made it difficult for enemy planes to find their targets. Traffic lights and car headlights were fitted with covers to keep them dim. Pedestrians were told to leave their white shirt-tails hanging out so they could be seen by car drivers at night!

In the countryside, some farmers painted white stripes on their cows to make sure they would be seen in a car's dim headlights.

People might think you're a zebra crossing!

Moo!

Deadly darkness

Blackouts were ideal cover for criminals and murderers. In 1942, a killer prowled the darkened London streets. The so-called 'Blackout Ripper' murdered women at night. After one attack, he ran off when a delivery boy saw him — leaving behind a gas mask case. It was traced to Gordon Cummins. The 27-year-old RAF serviceman was arrested.

I wish I hadn't left my ID number on my gas mask case!

More evidence was discovered and Cummins was found guilty of murdering four women. He was hanged at Wandsworth Prison, London, during an air raid, on 25th June, 1942.

Hitler  the Soap

Episode 3: Bunker Bathtime

Scene 1: Churchill's Bunker, London. Winston Churchill is in his bath while on the phone to US President Roosevelt. Date: 1942.

Action

Churchill:	How is it going, Franklin?
Roosevelt:	Since the Japanese attacked US ships at Pearl Harbor, we've been in this war up to our ears.
Churchill:	Just like me with these soapsuds…
Roosevelt:	Our troops are in Britain and I'm sending more to the desert in Africa…
Churchill:	Ah, that's too hot…
Roosevelt:	Sure, it's the desert.
Churchill:	I mean my bath water.
Roosevelt:	The Germans have a new tank called a 'Tiger'. It's wiping us out. We've gotta find out how it works.
Churchill:	Leave it with me, Franklin. Bye.

Scene 2: The desert in Tunisia. Date: 1943.

Major Liddel: I've captured a Tiger tank from the German army.

Churchill: Ah, where is the monster?

Liddel: I'm here, sir.

Churchill: Not you, the Tiger. Now, get that tank back to London. Make sure to keep this top secret.

Army engineers developed weapons to fight against the dreaded Tiger tank which helped change the course of the war. Yay!

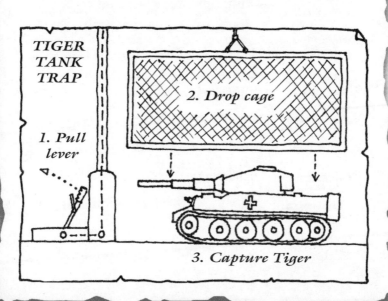

TIGER TANK TRAP

1. Pull lever

2. Drop cage

3. Capture Tiger

Hitler  the Soap

Episode 4: Hitler and Mussolini

Scene 1: Villa Gaggia, Feltre (northern Italy). Hitler and the Italian dictator, Benito Mussolini, are meeting. Date: July 1943.

Action

Hitler: Benito, you seem to be losing your nerve.

Mussolini: The war is not going well for either of us. You have been defeated in Russia and we've both lost battles in North Africa. Now the British...

Hitler: Don't mention the British. They stole one of my Tiger tanks. I am a furious fuming Führer!

Mussolini: My people are furious, too. They want bread, peace and freedom.

Hitler: Then shoot them.

Mussolini: I am losing the fight, Adolf. It is time to quit.

Hitler: Rubbish. Pull yourself together.

B-17 Flying Fortress

Soldier: A message for you, Il Duce, Sir. The Allies have taken Sicily and now they're bombing Rome.

Mussolini: I don't want this job any more. It's mad, bad and just too dangerous.

Days later

Is this the end for Mussolini?
Turn the page to find out...

Scene 2: The Italian people locked up Mussolini. Two months later, Italy surrendered the war.

Hitler: I am furious – again! I will send a commando team to rescue Benito. Then all will be tickety-boo.

So Mussolini was rescued ... only to be shot by his own people just over a year later. They hung him upside down from a lamp post. That really was the end of Mussolini.

And this is for taking us to war, Mussolini.

BANG!

Turn to page 78 for the next thrilling episode...

Danger — shark attack!

At the very end of the war (July 1945), a Japanese submarine fired torpedoes at the American warship USS *Indianapolis*. It sank quickly in shark-infested waters, but 900 of the crew jumped ship. They all bobbed on the waves in their life-jackets, waiting to be rescued. It took four days for a rescue ship to reach them. In that time, hundreds of sharks arrived to feed on the terrified survivors.

Only 317 men survived what was called 'the worst shark attack in history'.

It's a shame the war is about to end. I love these easy pickings!

SURVIVAL QUIZ 3

Team up with friends or try the quiz yourself to see if you would survive in World War II. Add up your scores for each answer. When you've done all the quizzes, check out the final results on page 88.

1. Are you scared of the dark?

A Absolutely

B Never

C Not really

2. Do you care if your shirt's not tucked in?

A Of course not

B Depends what I'm doing

C Yes — I like to look perfect

3. Do you like swimming in the sea?

A Not likely

B Whenever I can

C Sometimes

Scores for answers:

1. A = 1 B = 10 C = 8 (You'd have to get used to the dark in the war)

2. A = 10 B = 8 C = 0 (You couldn't worry about looking cool in the war — just safe!)

3. A = 10 B = 2 C = 5 (The sea could be dangerous — there weren't so many sharks, but there were lots of mines.)

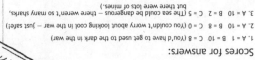

Chapter 5
MAD Medicine

Bomb blasts, fires, crashing planes and gunfire caused horrific injuries during the war. Not just soldiers, but ordinary people suffered shrapnel wounds, terrible burns, severed limbs, blood loss and serious head injuries. Hospitals had to act fast to find better ways to treat so many casualties. During World War II new drugs and medical ideas were developed. Many seemed crazy, but mad times can bring better medicine!

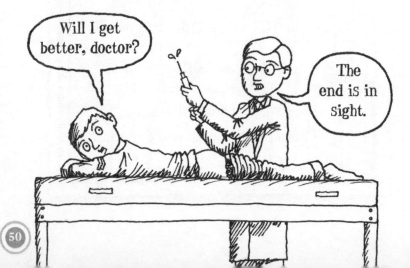

Will I get better, doctor?

The end is in sight.

When war-wounds weren't
dressed but neglected,

They'd often get badly
infected.

The cure? Never fear...

Just a jab in the rear

Yeow! That may not be what
you expected!

(A shot of penicillin was
beginning to work wonders.)

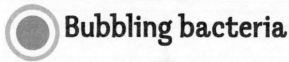

Bubbling bacteria

Infected war wounds could lead to deadly blood poisoning. The US Army gave every soldier a packet of powder called Sulfanilamide to sprinkle on wounds to stop infection. But this drug could cause nasty skin rashes so something new was needed.

Before the war, Scottish scientist Alexander Fleming was working with bacteria in his lab and left a dish of it on his bench by mistake. Mould began to grow inside the dish and killed the bacteria. Fleming was amazed! From this he developed penicillin — an antibiotic for fighting infections.

This penicillin will save millions of lives now and forever!

Mouse power

An Australian scientist, Howard Florey, tested penicillin on eight mice injected with deadly bacteria. Only four of the mice were treated with penicillin. The next day, the treated mice had recovered but the untreated mice were dead. This 'wonder drug' helped to save the lives of thousands of soldiers.

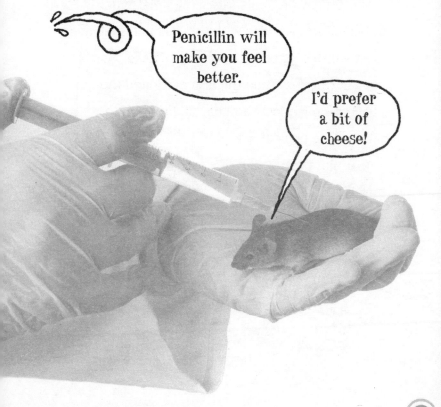

Daring doctor

Aircraft crews were often burnt in crashes. Surgeon Archibald McIndoe tried new ways of treating bad burns. He cut healthy skin from one part of a patient's body and 'planted' it over the burn, but often the new skin died from lack of blood supply. So McIndoe attached the new skin to another part of the body to keep it alive. In time, the new skin began to grow on its own.

McIndoe's patients formed a club called 'The Guinea Pig Club' because of McIndoe's experiments on them.

Nose job

Jack Toper suffered bad facial burns when his plane was shot down in 1943. McIndoe gave him a skin graft from his arm to his nose. He lifted a long flap of skin from Joe's arm up to his nose so new skin would begin to grow. McIndoe later cut the skin from Jack's arm to leave a healthy new nose.

I've picked a new nose!

Lobotomy madness

Stress and brain injuries saw a big rise in mental illness in World War II. A US doctor called Walter Freeman developed an operation called a 'lobotomy' to help with mental illness. While the patient was awake, he poked a sharp instrument into their brain through the eye socket and wiggled it about. He could do 250 lobotomies in a day! After lots of research, lobotomies were eventually banned as dangerous and dodgy surgery.

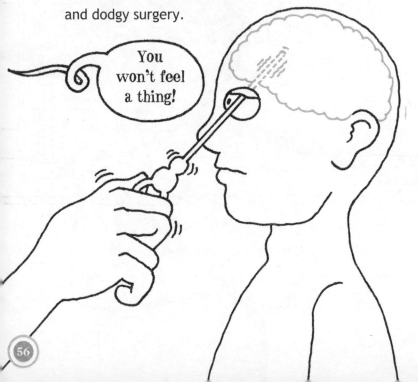

Blood rush

Another American idea seemed crazy at first, but it was a life-saver. In 1940, American doctor Charles Drew set up a system to collect blood from donors in New York City to export to British hospitals.

The blood was packed in ice and flown to field hospitals close to the fighting. Many injured soldier's lives were saved by Dr Drew's amazing blood transfusion service.

Team up with friends or try the quiz yourself to see if you would survive in World War II. Add up your scores for each answer. When you've done all the quizzes, check out the final results on page 88.

1. Have you ever needed to take antibiotics?

A I'm not sure

B Never

C Definitely

2. Do you like to look at yourself in the mirror?

A Of course not

B I don't really care

C Yes – I like to look perfect

3. Have you ever had an operation in hospital or needed extra blood?

A Yes

B No

C Possibly

Scores for answers:

1. A = 5 B = 10 C = 1 (Such medicines weren't available much at the start of the war)

2. A = 10 B = 8 C = 1 (Some burns victims couldn't bear to look at themselves)

3. A = 1 B = 9 C = 5 (Such treatment may not have been available early in the war)

Chapter 6

BAD and Beastly

Animals had a tough time in World War II. Pets were killed in air raids, and many zoo animals had to be shot in case they escaped during the attacks. But some animals had dangerous jobs to do. The armed forces used dogs, horses, pigeons and other animals for all kinds of daring work — including carrying bombs.

Private Monty at your service.

You may think it's madness
to mention

That the war saw a
secret invention...

A number of creatures

Had redesigned features...

KABOOM!

Oops – that was definitely
not the intention (yet).

Pigeon power

Pigeons were used to carry secret coded messages. Pigeon Joe flew 32 kilometres in 20 minutes (96.5 kph!) from British Army HQ to deliver a message just in time to save the lives of at least 100 Allied soldiers. They were about to get bombed by their own planes. Joe's message meant they got out fast!

I've just delivered a secret message to Hitler ... on top of his head!

Hee hee!

Hee hee!

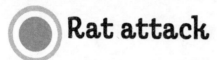

Rat attack

Some bright spark had a wacky ratty idea. It was to hide dead rats packed with explosives inside German coal bunkers. The rats would then get thrown with the coal into boilers and KABOOM!

You want me to do what????

The first batch of rat bombs was sent to Germany but the Germans smelt a rat! They found the rat bombs in their coal and the secret was blown.

Duh!

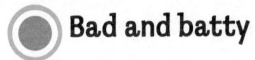

Bad and batty

The US Navy strapped bombs to thousands of bats at an airbase in New Mexico. The plan was to send them to bomb Japan. But the bats had other plans. They escaped and headed to a nice dark space under a fuel tank and KABOOM! Within minutes the airbase had gone up in flames — including a general's car. Oops.

Talk about a totally batty idea!

Danger! Dogs!

Dogs were trained for all sorts of dangerous work in World War II. When US troops invaded Sicily in 1943, dog hero Chips and his handler were pinned down on the beach by an Italian machine-gun team. Chips broke from his handler and attacked the gunners who ran off and surrendered!

I've got so many medals I'm more decorated than a Christmas tree!

Chips was awarded:
- Distinguished Service Cross
- Silver Star for bravery
- Purple Heart medal for wounds received in action

Look away now!

Other dogs carried out more deadly missions.
Russians trained dogs to carry bombs on their
backs and run under German tanks. A lever
sticking up from the dog's back would hit the tank
and set off the bomb — blowing up the tank and
the dog.

To train the dogs, food was put under Russian
tanks and the dogs learned to run under them.
But German tanks looked different, so many of
the dogs ran away from them and dived under
their own tanks instead. Hmm, bad plan!

Bad and sad

Many pets suffered when air raids destroyed their homes or killed their owners. One Italian dog, called Fido, was found injured by Carlo Soriani. Carlo nursed him back to health. From then on, Fido followed Carlo to the bus stop and greeted him on his return from work each evening. After two years, Carlo was killed at work in an air raid. For the next 14 years, Fido returned to the bus stop in the hope of seeing his master again — until he died in 1958.

Maybe this evening then!

That's so sad!

Pass the tissues...

SURVIVAL QUIZ 5

Team up with friends or try the quiz yourself to see if you would survive in World War II. Add up your scores for each answer. When you've done all the quizzes, check out the final results on page 88.

1. Do you like going to zoos?

A You bet

B Never

C Sometimes

2. Do you fancy handling pigeons?

A No, thanks

B I'm not too bothered

C Yes — they're cute

3. Are you a dog-lover?

A No

B Definitely

C A bit

Scores for answers:

1. A = 1 B = 10 C = 5 (Most zoos closed during the war)

2. A = 1 B = 6 C = 9 (250,000 pigeons were used in the UK so you'd need to look out for them)

3. A = 9 B = 2 C = 5 (There are many sad stories about dogs during the war)

Chapter 7
DANGEROUSLY Daring

Many of the missions of World War II were crazy. That's because heroes were ready to risk life and limb to stop Nazi plans. Anyone daring enough to spy or fly behind enemy lines knew they risked being captured and tortured by the Gestapo. To lift people's spirits, cinemas showed films with dashing film stars playing war heroes who always looked super-cool during the scariest danger.

Parachuting really messes up my hair!

With gunfire and sirens
all blaring,

Cool heroes of war were
so daring.

How very courageous

To be so outrageous

And mess up their hair
without caring!

Wow POW

More than 170,000 British prisoners of war were locked up during World War II. Many ended up at the dreaded 'escape-proof' Colditz Castle.

Peter Allan was determined to escape from Colditz. He dressed as a member of Hitler Youth and hid inside a mattress that was about to be loaded on a truck. Dumped in an empty house nearby, he cut himself out and climbed from a window. A German officer stopped his car and gave Peter a lift to Vienna. Days later Peter was arrested and ended up back at Colditz!

As prison camps go, Colditz is top of the range!

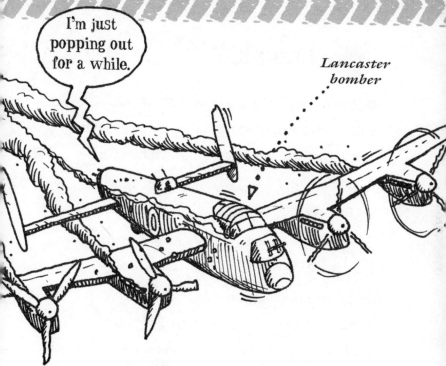

Lancaster bomber

I'm just popping out for a while.

Scary sky dive

Fancy leaping from a plane without a parachute?
Nicholas Alkemade was a rear gunner in an RAF
Lancaster bomber over Germany in 1944. Enemy
aircraft attacked his plane, which burst into flames
and fell from the sky. His parachute was burnt, so
Nicholas chose to jump to a quick death, rather
than burn. He fell 5,500 metres to the ground
below. Amazingly, pine trees and snow broke his
fall. He hobbled away with only a sprained leg!

I spies...

During the war, many daring spies were at work both in Nazi occupied countries and in Britain. Spies often had to use cunning disguises. Rumours spread that Nazi spies were landing in England dressed as nuns!

Super spy

Violette Bushell was born in England and married a French man, Captain Szabo, who was killed by the Nazis. Violette offered to help agents in France spy on German troops and parachuted into France. The Nazis captured her and she was tortured by the Gestapo, but she told them nothing. They shot her for being a spy just before the war ended.

Spies, such as Violette Szabo, hid secret messages in toothpaste inside toothpaste tubes!

D-Day madness

D-Day was 6th June, 1944. It was the day of the biggest invasion anywhere in the world... ever...

Allied forces planned to storm ashore onto French beaches in Normandy, fight the German army and advance towards Germany. The numbers were staggering:

- 4,000 ships poured 150,000 Allied troops and 50,000 vehicles on to the beaches.

- 23,000 troops parachuted from over 800 of the 13,000 planes flying over.

- Bombers pounded German troops, roads and bridges.

- Thousands of soldiers were killed in the battles.

Cunning plan

To fool German troops, Britain parachuted
hundreds of uniformed dummies further along the
coast from the real invasion. The German troops
rushed to fire on the dummies, which meant that
the real troops could land safely. Clever!

Zee Brits look
a right bunch
of dummies.

Hitler  *the Soap*

Episode 5: Assassination Plot

Scene 1: Hitler's 'Wolf's Lair' HQ, East Prussia.
General Stauffenberg has plotted with other generals to
blow up Hitler so that they can choose another leader.
Date: 20th July, 1944.

Action

Hitler:	Gentlemen, I changed this meeting to start early just in case there are assassins amongst us. Ha, ha, ha! Claus, you seem to be sweating. Anything the matter?
Stauffenberg:	*(Nervously clutching his case with a bomb inside)* Nein, mein Führer.
Hitler:	Then put that case down and we can begin.
Stauffenberg:	Certainly, Führer. Er … would you excuse me one moment? *(Exits and runs like mad)*
Heinz Brandt:	*(Moving the case with the bomb inside on the other side of a heavy table leg)* Allow me to move this case out of your way, Führer.

BANG!

Autsch! (Ouch!)

The table leg saved Hitler's life. Four others were killed. Hitler ordered the execution of anyone involved in the plot. About 7,000 people were arrested and many were executed, including the key plotters Stauffenberg, Olbricht and Beck.

Team up with friends or try the quiz yourself to see if you would survive in World War II. Add up your scores for each answer. When you've done all the quizzes, check out the final results on page 88.

1. Are you scared of heights?

A Don't even mention it

B Never

C It all depends

2. Would you ask a nun if she was a spy?

A Of course not

B If she looked odd

C Only if she had a moustache

3. What would you do if you saw a dummy on a parachute?

A Ignore it

B Report it

C Take it home to meet the family

Scores for answers:

1. A = 1 B = 9 C = 5 (You'd have to get used to heights in the Air Force)
2. A = 0 B = 9 C = 7 (You'd be wise to keep a look out for spies in disguise)
3. A = 0 B = 10 C = 1 (You should report it as it may be something dodgy)

Chapter 8
And Finally...

The war was coming to an end. In May 1945,
Allied forces reached Berlin and the Nazis were
beaten. Hitler refused to surrender so he and his
most trusted officers fled to his bunker. Here, in
underground rooms beneath Berlin, he celebrated
his 56th birthday and married Eva Braun. But his
last days, like the final days of the war itself,
were full of mad shocks and mysteries...

I got the
part of Blondi,
Hitler's dog.
Just my luck!

Hitler  the Soap

Episode 6: Defeat and Victory

Scene: Hitler's bunker under the Reich Chancellery in Berlin. Date: April, 1945.

Action

Hitler: *(Shouting)* Everyone is turning against me. Himmler has surrendered to the Allies.

Göebbels: I will never desert you, Führer. My wife and six children will stay here with you in your bunker.

Eva: Adolf, I will never leave you.

Hitler: I should hope not. We only got married yesterday. I have a present for you. It's a cyanide pill. I tested them on Blondi and her puppies and now they are dead *(sob)*. We have one each. We can't let them take us alive…

Eva: Hmph! Some honeymoon this is. I should have known it was going to end like this…

After Hitler and Eva killed themselves, Göebbels poisoned his children, his wife and then himself. Two days later, Germany surrendered. The war in Europe was over.

Final horror

Japanese troops still kept on fighting even though US forces were beating them in many battles. Japanese kamikaze, or suicide pilots, packed their planes with explosives and flew them into American ships. Over 2,500 Japanese pilots killed themselves and about 5,000 Allied sailors.

I'm useless at this kamikaze stuff – this is my third mission!

Atomic bomb

To force Japan's surrender, the US dropped an atom bomb on the Japanese city of Hiroshima.

Despite huge destruction, Japan's leaders still refused to surrender so another atom bomb was dropped on the city of Nagasaki. Japan eventually agreed to sign the surrender on 2nd September, 1945. After six years, World War II was finally over.

Ghostly goings-on

There are many ghost stories from World War II. In 1981, in Bethnal Green underground station in London, a station master working alone in the office late at night heard children crying. The cries grew louder … so did women's screams. He was sure they were the cries of 170 people who were crushed to death when they rushed into the station after hearing air-raid sirens.

Aarrggh!

Ghost plane?

Lindholm Park, an airfield in Yorkshire, sent Wellington bombers on air raids to Berlin. One night a returning plane crashed at the end of the runway, killing its Polish crew. Years later, stories were told of a figure in pilot's uniform asking locals in Polish for the way home. On the nights the pilot appeared, people saw a crashed Wellington's tail section rise up from the mist. Eeek — don't have nightmares!

What is your total score from the SURViVAL quizzes at the end of the chapters? Add up your points from all 18 questions to see how well you might survive in World War II.

Over 150	WOW — you'd make a great war-time survivor! Your chances of making it to old age are promising. Then again, were all your answers strictly honest?
100 — 150	Fairly good. You're a war-time survivor with a fair chance of reaching middle age with a smile under your gas mask.
80 — 100	Not bad. You'd make a fairly average war-time survivor but don't plan for old age.
50 — 80	Oo-er — you're high risk. War-time isn't for you. You have seriously low survival chances.
Below 50	AAH! Give up now. You wouldn't make a successful war-time anything! Only a miserably dead one.

If your scores were a whole mixture, that means you'd probably be fairly normal. You'd have no idea if or when something nasty would strike … like sharing a night in an air-raid shelter with cold spam fritters and a rat in a gas mask. In fact, the horrid Heinrich Himmler himself might already have your name and be about to send the Gestapo to get you...

Dramatic Dates

September 1939	Germany invades Poland. Britain and France declare war on Germany.
April 1940	Germany invades Norway and Denmark.
May 1940	Germany invades Belgium and the Netherlands. Germany invades France.
September 1940	Germany bombs Britain – the London Blitz begins.
June 1941	Germany invades the Soviet Union.
September 1941	Mass murder of Jewish people at Auschwitz begins.
December 1941	Japan bombs Pearl Harbor. The US declares war on Japan.
1942	Japan captures the Philippines and Burma.
June 1942	The Allies defeat Japan in the Battle of Midway.

June 1942	British and Indian forces fight the Japanese in Burma.
May 1943	Axis troops in North Africa surrender. Italy surrenders.
September 1943	D-day: Allied troops land in France to invade Europe.
July 1944	Operation Valkyrie bomb plot to kill Hitler almost succeeds.
August 1944	Paris is liberated from German control.
October 1944	Japan's navy is defeated near the Philippines.
April 1945	Italy's dictator Mussolini is assassinated. Two days later, Hitler and his wife commit suicide in their bunker in Berlin.
May 1945	Germany surrenders – the end of World War II in Europe.
August 1945	Atom bombs are dropped on Hiroshima and Nagasaki.
September 1945	Japan surrenders – World War II ends after six years.

Gruesome Glossary

air-raid siren a loud blaring alarm that sounded as a warning before an air-raid attack

air raids attacks by aircraft (bombers) on targets on the ground

allied countries (the Allies) the countries that fought with Britain against the Axis powers

antibiotics drugs that kill the harmful germs and bacteria that cause disease

assassins people who kill a leader or an important person

Axis countries countries, such as Germany, Italy and Japan, that fought against the Allies

blood transfusion taking blood from one person's body and putting it into another to replace blood lost during surgery or from serious injury

bunker a concrete shelter made under ground to protect people against attack

D-Day 6th June, 1944 – the day Allied forces landed in northern France to begin setting European countries free from German occupation

deranged mad or insane

dictator a ruler who has total authority; one who is often cruel or brutal

dog-fight a battle at close range between fighter planes

extermination camps a place where people were sent to be gassed

field hospitals temporary hospitals set up near a battle zone to give emergency care

Flying Fortress a four-engine heavy bomber aircraft

Führer the title given to Adolf Hitler, meaning 'leader' or 'guide' in German

Il Duce the name given by Italians to their leader Benito Mussolini, meaning 'The Leader'

kamikaze pilots Japanese air force pilots sent on suicide missions

maiden young unmarried girl

Nazi Party the extreme political group that ruled Germany from 1933 to 1945

refugees people forced to leave their country to escape war

Reich Chancellery massive building that was the centre for Hitler's government in Berlin

shrapnel sharp metal pieces that shoot out from an exploded bomb or mine

swede a root vegetable

Third Reich the rule of the Nazi Party in Germany between 1933 and 1945

Tiger tank a German tank built from 1942 to 1944 and used to destroy enemy aircraft and tanks. It has a very powerful 8 mm gun and thick armour

turnip a root vegetable

War Cabinet a group of people formed by a government in war-time to help decide on how to fight the war

Weird Websites

Pssst. There's something you need to know. This book is a fun look at just some of the mad, bad and dangerous WWII goings-on. For more facts, feats and daring-dos take a peep at:

www.ducksters.com/history/world_war_ii/
Check this out for homework and school projects

www.bbc.co.uk/schools/primaryhistory/world_war2/
Test your WWII know how

www.youtube.com/watch?v=ckicPSty7Pw
Would you wake up Adolf Hitler?

http:/www.youtube.com/watch?v=8uxAopLZW74
Join in a jolly sing song with WWII pilots!

Infernal Index

Want to 'nose' what this is all about? Turn to page 55.

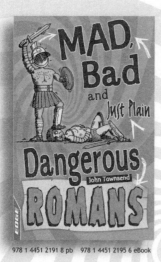

978 1 4451 2191 8 pb   978 1 4451 2195 6 eBook

978 1 4451 2192 5 pb   978 1 4451 2196 3 eBook

978 1 4451 2193 2 pb   978 1 4451 2239 7 eBook

978 1 4451 2194 9 pb   978 1 4451 2240 3 eBook